Also by Patrick McKeown

The Oxygen Advantage
The Simple, Scientifically Proven Technique to a Healthier, Slimmer, Faster, and Fitter You

Asthma Free Naturally

Anxiety Free: Stop Worrying and Quieten Your Mind

Sleep with Buteyko: Stop Snoring, Sleep Apnoea and Insomnia

Close Your Mouth: Buteyko Clinic Manual

Buteyko DVD set for High Blood Pressure, Fatigue, Insomnia, Chronic Hyperventilation, Snoring, and Sleep Apnoea

Buteyko Kids Meet Dr Mew DVD set

Buteyko Mindfulness Method DVD set

"Be who you are
and say what you feel,
because those who mind don't matter
and those who matter
don't mind."

Dr. Seuss

Always Breathe Correctly

*Complete Self-Help Manual to Unblock the Nose,
Stop Mouth Breathing, Control Asthma,
Improve Concentration and Develop a Perfect Face
with Straight Teeth*

by Patrick McKeown

Always Breathe Correctly: Complete Self-Help Manual to Unblock the Nose, Stop Mouth Breathing, Control Asthma, Improve Concentration and Develop a Perfect Face with Straight Teeth

is the new expanded and revised version of
Always Breathe Correctly

First published as *ABC to be Asthma Free*
in 2004 by Asthma Care

Revised 2011, 2015

Web: www.ButeykoClinic.com
Email: info@ButeykoClinic.com

Published in the U.S. by Carol Baglia, RRT 2011

© Patrick McKeown 2004, 2015

ISBN-13: 978-0956682314

All rights reserved.
No part of this publication may be copied, reproduced or transmitted in any form or by any means, without permission in writing from the publishers. This book is sold subject to the condition that it shall not, by way of trade or otherwise, be lent, re-sold or otherwise circulated without the publishers prior consent, in any form of binding or cover other than that in which it is published and without similar condition including this condition, being imposed on the publisher

My Magic Breathing Book

Hello! I'm David 1

Tumbletown's summer sports day 2

Argo the wizard 3

Always...Breathe...Correctly... 4

Magic works in 1, 2, 3 6

Quiet as a mouse 8

My nose has magic 12

Everyone knows 13

That's why we all have noses 14

Your teeth will be straight and true 16

The magic spot 17

Pop! 18

An ice cream wafer 19

A big grin 20

Stick out your tongue 21

Use ABC 22

Another magic secret 23

Step 2 24

Counting 25

Steps are FUN! 26
Every day 27
Big breaths 28
Hear your breathing 29
How to breathe 31
Remember your ABC and 1...2...3 32
Sports day 33
Argo appears 35
Just in time 36
Friends laughed 37
Harder and faster 38
How did he do it? 39
Easy like 1, 2, 3 40
Share the magic of ABC 42
The wise wizard's special note of caution 48
Why breathe through the nose? 49
Motivating children 53
About the author 54

Note:

The therapeutic procedures in this book are based on the training, experience and research of the author. The information contained in this book is not intended to serve as a replacement for professional medical advice. This book teaches the importance of breathing through the nose, how to practise simple breathing exercises and adopt lifestyle guidelines aimed at promoting good health. Do not change or alter medications without the consent of a registered physician. The author and the publisher specifically disclaim any and all liability arising directly or indirectly from the use or application of any information contained in this book.

"Hello! I'm David," said the little boy.

He is sad because he would love to run and play with his friends, but he can't because David breathes through his mouth and running makes him cough and wheeze.

It slows him down and makes him tired, and although David takes big gulps of air, he still feels tired and breathless.

Every day on his walk to school, David sees a sign for Tumbletown's Summer Sports Day and the race to find out the fastest runner.

It makes David sad because he would love to run and race his friends, so he makes a wish to cheer himself up.

"I wish I could run a race this summer," says David.

That night, just before David falls asleep, a wizard appears and whispers into his ear:

"I am **Argo the Wizard** and I can make your wish come true."

David coughs and is so surprised.

But the wizard's whisper is soft and gentle and Argo says: "It's as easy as ABC to make your wish come true - because the ABC game is all you need to do."

"What game is that?" asks David, and the wizard whispers back, "it's magic that will help you run...and much, much more!"

"The ABC game will help your face and teeth grow true and can even help make a cleverer you!"

"And what's best of all is that it is so easy...because the ABC game is Always...Breathe...Correctly!"

When David woke up in the morning he remembered Argo but thought, "I must have been dreaming."

But suddenly the wizard appeared and smiled and whispered, "You're wide awake now David, but last night you didn't play the ABC game when you were sleeping."

Rubbing his eyes with surprise David said "But I don't know how to."

"I know ABC is Always…Breathe… Correctly…but please Argo, you must teach me."

Argo magically made a piece of paper appear,
and pointing to the words, said,

"See, it really is easy like ABC… and the magic works
in 1, 2, 3."

"One is to breathe through your nose both night and day,
making sure your tongue's tip does not stray from the
magic spot at the roof of your mouth, behind your teeth,
up there at the top."

"Two is to practise the magic Steps every day, and three
is to breathe gently and in the quietest way."

David tried to play the ABC game all day, remembering
1, 2, and 3 just like the wizard did say.

But despite his best efforts his nose kept feeling blocked and stuffy and David said to himself,

"I thought ABC was supposed to be easy!"

"It is!" said Argo, suddenly appearing again, "you just need to know how to unblock your nose!"

So with a whisper the wizard shared the magic Steps with David, softly saying in his ear...

"Sit down and quiet as a mouse take a small breath in and out through your nose."

SSSSHHHHH...

"Now with your fingers, pinch your nostrils closed so no air comes in, and no air goes out."

"And as you're holding your nose closed,
start gently nodding your head up and down
    for as long as you can.
When you need to,
    just let go of your nose, and
slowly, quiet as a mouse
    breathe in through your nose
and let no air sneak in through your mouth.
Wait for about 30 seconds and practise again."

"Do it three times," said Argo, "and your nose won't be blocked."
"But what if it is?" asked David, and the wizard replied,

"Like all magic, you have to keep practising until you get it right."

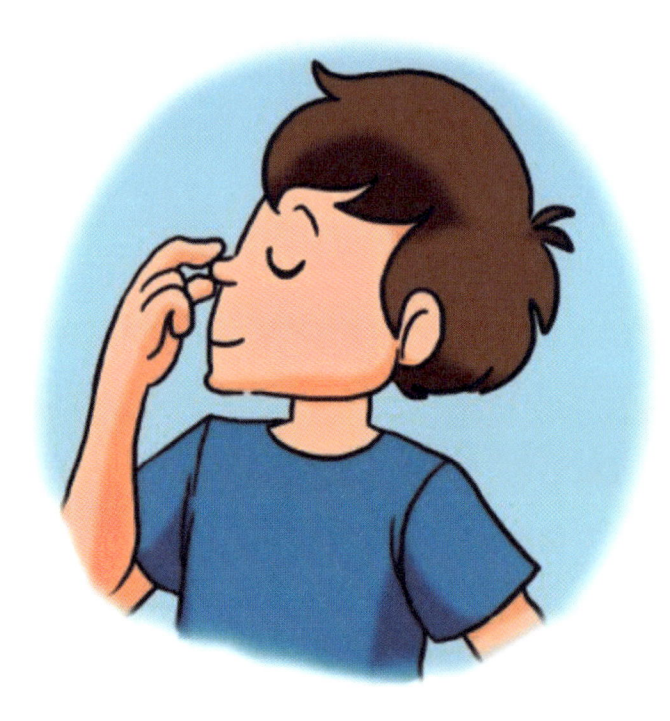

"So keep practising David and make your wish come true - breathe out of your nose, pinch your nostrils and nod your head until the block goes."

"And what if it comes back?" asked David, and the wizard whispered his answer...

The Secret To All Magic

"**The secret to all magic is** to practise again!"

"The nose has lots of magic," said Argo, "and all you have to do to use it – is to breathe properly through it!"

"My nose has magic?" asked David, who was getting excited.

"Yes," said Argo. "Your nose stops dirty air from getting inside and nibbling at your body."

"It cleans the air and warms it up for us.
And it's really important you breathe through it, because only then can the magic work."

The kind wizard looked at David and whispered:

"Everyone knows that we use our Eyes for seeing..."

"Everyone knows we use our Ears for listening.
Everyone knows we use our Mouths for
talking and eating and drinking..."

"But!" and here the wizard's whisper got louder...

"not everyone knows about the magic when we only use our Nose for breathing!"

"Is the magic
to do with smelling?",
asked David,
"because I use my nose for that."

"Sometimes," said Argo, smiling.
"But the real magic is
all to do with breathing."

"Always and only through my
nose!" said David.

"Exactly!" said the wizard.
"That's why we all have noses!"

The whispering wizard looked at the boy and said, "David, I am going to tell you another secret, told to me by a famous, friendly dentist."

"If you breathe through your mouth
and not through your nose,
your teeth will be crooked
and your face can grow
long and narrow."

As Argo spoke he made appear another piece of magic paper.

"Look," whispered the wizard, "look at what happened to the boy who kept his mouth open when he was a child."

The wizard wiggled his fingers over the drawing and whispered...

"Look David, see the magic that happens when you breathe through your nose with the tip of your tongue resting on the magic spot in the roof of your mouth..."

As Argo's fingers wiggled, the drawing changed, and the wizard whispered,

"You will grow the perfect face and your teeth will be straight and true."

"Please Argo, show me where the magic spot is," said David, and the wizard replied...

"To find it, all you need is to first make the sound of 'N'."
"Ennn," said David.

"Perfect!" said Argo. "Now your tongue is resting behind but not touching your top front teeth. Slowly bring the rest of your tongue up into the roof of your mouth - that's where the mouth's magic spot is."

"Use it David," whispered Argo. "Always keep the tip of your tongue on the magic spot and always ask yourself: "Is my mouth closed? Is my tongue on the magic spot?"

"Ennnnn," said David, practising with his tongue to find the magic spot. "I don't know if I can find it, is there another way Argo?"

The wizard smiled and made the sound of a big full "pop!"

"What's that?" said David.
"That's another way to find the magic spot," said the wise wizard. "Just make the sound of 'pop!' Just place your tongue in the roof of your mouth and quickly move it down to make the sound..."

"Pop!" went David.

"That's it," said Argo. "The magic spot is where you placed your tongue in the roof of your mouth before you went 'pop!'"

David made the sound again and the wizard smiled and said: "Practise ten 'pops' three times a day because it really helps your ABC and will help make your wish come true."

David said "Ennnnn," and then went "Pop!"
And Argo watched and whispered:

"David, when you keep your tongue on the magic spot and breathe through your nose as quiet as a mouse, do you feel your swallowing is different?"

David nodded and the wizard wiggled his fingers...and all of a sudden an ice cream wafer appeared.
"Look David, you can use this to practise how to swallow - just break off a little piece about the size of your thumb and chew it very gently - don't eat it! - just chew until you turn it into a tiny soft ball."

"Now curl your tongue into the shape of a hollow and hold the wafer-ball near the front. Put the tip of your tongue on the 'N' spot, close your teeth and slide your tongue's tip up and back and press it firmly against the skin on the roof of your mouth, away from your teeth."

"Now you can swallow and try to suck at the same time."

"If you do it right you will feel your teeth bite together."

"Hold your lips apart and make a big grin because this helps the tongue rise-up and stops the lips being involved in the swallow."

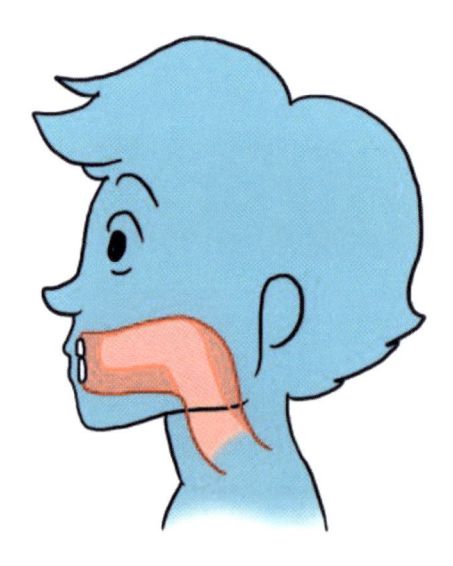

David tried as the wizard said, and Argo watched and whispered, "practise until you feel it working - you'll know it is when your face doesn't show that you are swallowing."

"Ask your mommy or daddy for help or use a mirror to watch yourself and then stick out your tongue and check that none of the wafer is left on it."

"What if I don't have an ice cream wafer?" asked David.

Argo smiled.

"You can use a small piece of bread," said the wizard, "just remember to practise and make sure that from now on your tongue is in the magic spot in the roof of your mouth every time you swallow."

David practised every day, always trying to remember. When he forgot... Argo appeared and whispered "ABC" into David's ear.

"When watching TV use ABC. When walking home or to school and in class always remember ABC, and when doing your homework and helping with chores, use ABC at home and when you're outdoors!"

"And can ABC help silence snores?" asked David.
"Yes, of course," said Argo.
"ABC magic works all day and night."

David practised ABC so much that he didn't breathe through his mouth at all anymore.

It made Argo so very happy that he decided to share with David another magic secret to help with his wish.

The wizard whispered, "Do you remember Steps 1, 2, 3? Now it's time to do Step 2 with me."

"Take a small breath in through your nose, then breathe a small breath out through your nose."

"Hold your nose so that the air does not enter or escape and see how many steps you can walk without breathing in."

David and the wizard walked together and Argo whispered, "Step 2 is 'the Steps'.

"When you really need to breathe in, let go of your nose...and then breathe in through your nose...and try and calm your breathing as quickly as possible."

"Then rest for one minute and do 'the Steps' again."

To help David practise, Argo gave him a special chart so he can count the two lines of Steps that he does every day.

After one cycle of Steps – holding his nose and counting how many he can do before he needs to breathe in through his nose again – David rests for a minute and goes again.

And then again until he's done all six.

Then later on in the day David completes line 2, holding his nose and counting how many Steps he can do…

Each time he tries to get a higher number – sometimes he can't and sometimes he can!

"Steps are fun!"
said David.

"Just like ABC!"

You can see and use for yourself Argo's chart – it's at the end of this book – but make sure you read the **Wise Wizard's Special Note of Caution** because magic is powerful and must be done right!

Every day Argo the wizard appears to David and whispers "ABC." And every time David hears it he repeats his Steps.

And when he forgets to keep his mouth closed or his tongue on the magic spot, Argo appears and whispers,

"Always remember to A...B...C."

David practises and is able to do more and more Steps each week and wise wizard Argo is happy.

"David you have done so well
so now it's time for me to tell
the last 1...2...3
of the magic game
that's ABC!"

The wizard whispered
slightly louder...

"Big breathing makes the mouth open,
big breathing blocks the nose
and causes coughs and wheezing."

"AND BIG BREATHS
LEAVE YOU BREATHLESS!"

"But how do I know when I'm breathing big?" asked David.
"Anytime you can hear yourself breathing, then you are breathing big" answered Argo.
"If you can hear your breath when you are sitting down or when you're trying to sleep in bed, or when your mouth is open, then David, you are breathing big."

Argo blows a big breath of air onto David's hand.
"This is big breathing," the wizard whispers.
"A dinosaur breathes the same way."

Argo blows a tiny breath onto David's hand.

"This is ABC David – just like the breathing of a little mouse! ABC is quiet breathing, quiet like a mouse!"

"The mouse uses its little nose and quietly breathes tiny little breaths to hide from the cat," whispered Argo. "If the cat can hear the mouse, it will chase the mouse." "So breathe quietly David, breathe quiet as a little mouse hiding from the cat."

"I've never heard a little mouse breathe," said David. "Exactly!" said Argo.

"No, no," said David laughing.

"I mean I don't know HOW TO BREATHE like a mouse. Can you show me Argo, please?"

"It's easy to breathe like a little mouse," whispered the wizard. "Just put your finger under your nose and try and feel the warm air on it."

"Now breathe gently and softly so you don't feel the air on your finger at all!"

David imagines

he's a little white mouse

with his finger under

his nose

and breathes so quietly

and gently

that he cannot feel

the warm air

on his finger at all.

"I have one final piece of wisdom for you," Argo the wizard whispered to David.

"If you ever see dirty air that people call pollution, try not to let it into your body. Remember your ABC and 1...2...3 and breathe in, breathe out, take the Steps and hold your breath and walk away."

David practises his ABC and 1...2...3 every day
and feels so much better now that he doesn't feel tired and slow.

He sees the sign on his way to school and thinks about his wish to run a race with his friends.

The big Tumbletown Summer Sports Day arrives and David decides to sign up for the race.

But the other children don't know about the ABC and laugh and make fun of David because they think he will run and just cough and wheeze.

David hears them laughing and is afraid he will be too slow so he goes away and tries to hide.

Suddenly Argo appears and whispers, "A...B...C..." to David.

"You have practised well and can run the race David."

"And if you can do more than 80 Steps from number 2, you'll run very fast, so I have every faith in you!"

David remembered how he practised his ABC and 1, 2, 3, and how he started with only a few Steps, when he breathed out and stepped whilst holding his nose...

But, after practising two lines of Steps every day for two months, he was counting more than 80 and just in time for the race!

David's friends laughed when he lined up beside them.

But halfway through the race,

when all the boys and girls were running as fast as they could,

David was still there beside them.

"ABC" is easy as 1,2,3," he said to himself and suddenly...

David ran harder and faster...

...and beat all his friends to the line!

Everybody cheers with delight.
Argo the wizard is so happy.
David is great at running.

"HOW DID HE DO IT?" everyone asks.

"It's all because of the ABC Game," said David.

"A, B, C is ALWAYS BREATHE CORRECTLY!"

"And the best thing is that it's so easy, like 1...2...3!"

"Breathe only through your nose, all of the time, with your tongue on the magic spot, and practise Steps twice each day and if you can reach 80 you will be very fast when you play! "And don't forget - ABC means to breathe quietly and gently - just like a little mouse!"

"ABC has stopped my coughs and wheezing and now I'm not breathless and can run very fast with my friends!"

"And it will help my face to grow to its proper shape and keep my teeth all straight and true!"

"Just follow ABC and 1...2...3 and you can run as fast as me!"

Argo wants to share the magic of ABC with every boy and girl so he has written this especially for you.

"Remember ABC and every day and all during the night keep your mouth closed with your tongue on the magic spot. And every day practise two lines of Steps and remember to be quiet as a mouse when you're breathing."

"This boys and girls is the ABC and yes, it's easy like 1…2…3!"

Argo gave David a special chart so he could practise his Steps, and he has made one for you that your parents can photocopy to record your ABC progress.

Remember to read first the Wise Wizard's Special Note of Caution - because magic is powerful and must be done right!

Photocopy the next page and start recording your progress. Rest for one minute between each cycle of Steps. Two rows of Steps per day with at least two hours rest in between each line. Steps should be practised on an empty tummy.

My Step Diary

Date	My Steps	One Minute Rest	My Steps	One Minute Rest	My Steps	One Minute Rest	My Steps	One Minute Rest	My Steps	One Minute Rest	My Steps

My Step Diary

Date	My Steps	One Minute Rest	My Steps	One Minute Rest	My Steps	One Minute Rest	My Steps	One Minute Rest	My Steps	One Minute Rest	My Steps

My Step Diary

Date	My Steps	One Minute Rest	My Steps	One Minute Rest	My Steps	One Minute Rest	My Steps	One Minute Rest	My Steps	One Minute Rest	My Steps

My Step Diary

Date	My Steps	One Minute Rest	My Steps	One Minute Rest	My Steps	One Minute Rest	My Steps	One Minute Rest	My Steps	One Minute Rest	My Steps

The Wise Wizard's Special Note of Caution

Steps exercises are specifically aimed towards children and teenagers. By doing Steps, everyone will experience signs of health improvement including:

- fewer asthma symptoms
- less coughing
- less wheezing
- less nasal congestion
- increased calmness
- better sleep
- more energy
- improved dental health
- improved sports performance

While practising Steps is a perfectly safe exercise (similar to swimming underwater) it can involve an element of risk for some children with particular illnesses or susceptibilities.

Please note the following in particular:

- Your child or teenager should not commence Steps if they have any serious medical condition including any of the following: diabetes; severe asthma; epilepsy; any heart problems; a known tumour or kidney disease.
- If they experience an exacerbation of their symptoms, then they are not doing the exercises correctly and they should stop until it is established that they can do them correctly. If your child or teenager is having breathing difficulty, then do not do Steps. Steps exercises are only to be practised when no symptoms are present.

Why Breathe Through The Nose?

Nasal breathing is transformative - it improves sleep, concentration and sports performance, it helps to avoid bad breath and ensures normal development of the face and straight teeth.

Even though its primary functions are to filter, moisten and humidify incoming air before it is drawn into the body, the nose is often underused for the essential task of breathing. Many children and adults breathe through their mouths instead, either out of habit or because of nasal obstruction.

I too was a habitual mouth-breather, from childhood into my early twenties, bypassing my nose completely. My breathing habits went hand in hand with my respiratory issues, but despite being hospitalised for recurrent asthma attacks and the overwhelming evidence of the detrimental effects of mouth-breathing, I was never once told to breathe through my nose.

Instead, I accepted my constant snoring, fatigue, tension, stress, asthma, and poor concentration as part of who I was, without realising that all these issues and more could easily be helped with a few corrections to my breathing.

Prolonged mouth-breathing also caused an alteration to the structure of my face, resulting in a high upper palate, undeveloped jaws, smaller airways and crooked teeth. Little did I know the development of the lower half of the face and jaws is largely influenced by whether the mouth is open or closed during the formative years of childhood.

Not only does mouth-breathing lead to uneven teeth and disrupt growth of the face,[1-4] there is also much documented evidence showing that it is a significant factor in developing obstructive sleep apnoea,[5-9] a condition that is closely linked with high blood pressure, reduced quality of life and fatigue.

Nasal breathing, on the other hand, performs at least 30 functions on behalf of the body.[10] Along with providing a sense of smell, the nose is nature's way of preparing air before it enters the lungs. As the nostrils are much smaller than the mouth, they create approximately 50% more resistance in comparison to mouth breathing, resulting in a 10-20% greater oxygen uptake in the blood.[10] Breathing optimally through the nose not only increases blood oxygenation, but also increases the amount of oxygen delivered to tissues and organs.[10]

Having a stuffy nose adversely affects sleep both in children and adults. After a night spent breathing heavily through the mouth, a child will wake up exhausted, causing poor concentration and frustration at school. If this continues over a period of time, a psychological evaluation and possible diagnosis of ADD or ADHD may follow.[11]

When I speak to any parent who has a child labelled with ADD, my first piece of advice is to check their sleep habits.

- Are they breathing through their mouth?
- Are they twisting and turning during the night, waking up with the bed clothes tangled in the morning?
- Do they snore or hold their breath during sleep?
- Is their breathing audible during sleep?

Answering yes to any of these questions suggests that the child is suffering the detrimental effects of mouth breathing.

Nasal breathing is of the utmost importance if you wish to improve your child's quality of sleep.

Any adult will understand the knock-on effect of crankiness and frustration when they have a poor night's sleep – so how can a child face the day with boundless energy if their sleep is not right?

The good news is that sleep experts are becoming increasingly concerned about the impact of open mouth breathing during sleep, especially for children. Among these researchers is Dr Christian Guilleminault, a leading figure in the field of sleep medicine.

In the early 1970s, while working at the Stanford University Sleep Disorders Clinic, Dr Guilleminault monitored the blood pressure of sleeping patients and discovered that when patients held their breath during sleep, their blood pressure dramatically increased.

Since then, Dr Guilleminault has made many further discoveries in the field of sleep medicine. Among these, which I am delighted to include, is his recognition that: "the case against mouth breathing is growing, and given its negative consequences, we feel that restoration of the nasal breathing route as early as possible is critical."[12]

This paper, published in 2015, goes on to say that "restoration of nasal breathing during wake and sleep may be the only valid 'complete' correction of paediatric sleep disordered breathing."[12]

Notes:

1. Harari D, Redlich M, Miri S, Hamud T, Gross M. The effect of mouth breathing versus nasal breathing on dentofacial and craniofacial development in orthodontic patients. *Laryngoscope*.2010 Oct;(120(10)):2089-93

2. D'Ascanio L, Lancione C, Pompa G, Rebuffini E, Mansi N, Manzini M. Craniofacial growth in children with nasal septum deviation: A cephalometric comparative study. *International Journal of Pediatric Otorhinolaryngology*. October 2010;74(10):1180-1183

3. Baumann I, Plinkert PK. Effect of breathing mode and nose ventilation on growth of the facial bones. *HNO*.1996 May;(44(5)):229-34

4. Tourne LP. The long face syndrome and impairment of the nasopharyngeal airway. *The Angle Orthodontist*.1990 Fall;(60(3)):167-76

5. Kim EJ, Choi JH, Kim KW, Kim TH, Lee SH, Lee HM, Shin C, Lee KY, Lee SH. *The impacts of open-mouth breathing on upper airway space in obstructive sleep apnea: 3-D MDCT analysis.* Eur Arch Otorhinolaryngol. 2010 Oct 19.

6. Kreivi HR, Virkkula P, Lehto J, Brander P. *Frequency of upper airway symptoms before and during continuous positive airway pressure treatment in patients with obstructive sleep apnea syndrome.* Respiration. 2010;80(6):488-94.

7. Ohki M, Usui N, Kanazawa H, Hara I, Kawano K. *Relationship between oral breathing and nasal obstruction in patients with obstructive sleep apnea.* Acta Otolaryngol Suppl. 1996;523:228-30.

8. Lee SH, Choi JH, Shin C, Lee HM, Kwon SY, Lee SH. *How does open-mouth breathing influence upper airway anatomy?* Laryngoscope. 2007 Jun;117(6):1102-6

9. Scharf MB, Cohen AP *Diagnostic and treatment implications of nasal obstruction in snoring and obstructive sleep apnea.* Ann Allergy Asthma Immunol. 1998 Oct;81(4):279-87; quiz 287-90.

10. Timmons B.H., Ley R. *Behavioral and Psychological Approaches to Breathing Disorders*. 1st ed. . Springer; 1994

11. Jefferson Y: Mouth breathing: adverse effects on facial growth, health, academics and behaviour. General dentist.2010 Jan- Feb; 58 (1): 18-25

12. Lee SY, Guilleminault C, Chiu HY, Sullivan SS (2015) *Mouth breathing, nasal "disuse", and pediatric sleep-disordered-breathing.* In 'Sleep and Breathing' (2015) Stanford University Sleep Medicine Division, Stanford Outpatient Medical Center, Redwood City CA

Motivating Children

An integral part of helping children and teenagers to change their breathing habits is to explain why it is so important to breathe through the nose.

For example, nasal breathing will:

- improve sleep
- improve concentration
- improve sports performance
- help to avoid bad breath
- ensure normal development of the face and straight teeth

When I work with children and teens I ask them which reasons they consider to be most important for breathing through the nose.

The most popular replies tend to be improvements to athleticism and the development of a good looking face.

It is imperative not to highlight the negative features of mouth-breathing – such as set-back jaws or a narrow face. Instead, reassure your child of the many benefits of reduced nasal breathing on their health, and ensure they hold onto their beautiful faces.

About the author

Patrick McKeown is Clinical Director of Education and Training with Buteyko Clinic International.

To date, Patrick has written seven books and produced four DVD sets on the Buteyko Method, including three Amazon.com and Amazon.co.uk bestsellers:

Close Your Mouth, Asthma-Free Naturally, and *Anxiety Free: Stop Worrying and Quieten your Mind.*

The Buteyko self-help manual **Close Your Mouth** has been translated into ten different languages including French, German, Italian, Spanish, Norwegian and Russian. His latest book, **The Oxygen Advantage** improves sports performance by addressing dysfunctional breathing patterns and simulating high altitude training.

Patrick is a graduate of Trinity College Dublin and in 2002 he was accredited as a Buteyko breathing practitioner by the late Professor Konstantin Buteyko.

Having suffered from asthma, rhinitis and sleep-disordered breathing for over 20 years, Patrick is able to offer both theoretical knowledge and his own experiences to help clients overcome similar challenges.

You can contact Patrick by emailing Patrick@ButeykoClinic.com